An Italian Pantry

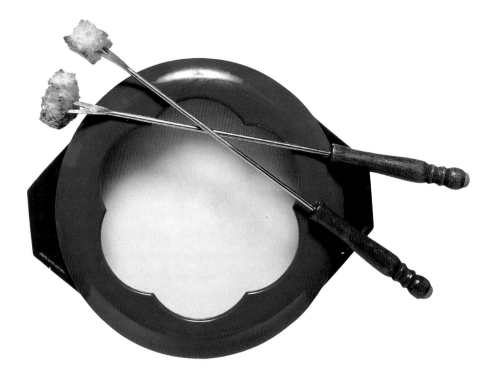

Cheese

Gabriella Ganugi

An Italian Pantry

WINE APPRECIATION GUILD

Also available in
"An Italian Pantry":

OLIVE OIL

PASTA

PROSCIUTTO

First Published in North America 2004
The Wine Appreciation Guild
360 Swift Avenue
South San Francisco CA 94080

ISBN 1-891267-69-8

This book was conceived, edited and designed by
McRae Books Srl, Florence, Italy.

Series Editor: Anne McRae
Text: Gabriella Ganugi
Photography: Marco Lanza
Set Design: Rosalba Gioffrè
Design: Marco Nardi
Editing: Anne McRae, Holly Willis

2 4 6 8 10 9 7 5 3 1

Color separations: Fotolito Toscana, Florence, Italy
Printed and bound in China

Contents

Introduction

This medieval miniature shows Ricotta being made. The earliest encyclopedic manual on cheese in Europe was compiled by Pantaleone da Confidenza and published in 1477. His detailed descriptions of Italian cheeses include many that are still on the market today, such as Fontina, Robiola, and Marzolino del Chianti.

In Italy, cheese is made from cow's milk, as well as from the milk of ewes, goats, and water buffalo.

The Italian word for cheese: *formaggio*, comes from the Latin *formaticum*, meaning "solidified milk." The origins of cheesemaking probably date back to the dawn of farming, when sheep, goats, and cattle were first kept and new methods for conserving food were invented. Cheese was a staple food for the ancient Greeks and Romans. In Roman times, cheese was served at most meals and its flavor was frequently enhanced with garlic, salt, fish, or eggs.

Cheese was also a popular food during the Middle Ages. According to legend, Attila the Hun ordered the preparation of a special cheese made from human milk, and it is said that Charlemagne discovered Roquefort cheese at a country monastery as he returned from a hunting trip. Production increased in medieval times, and records show that Parmesan, Gorgonzola, Mozzarella, and Pecorino (among others), were all being made by the 12th century.

Cheesemaking underwent profound changes as the Industrial Revolution took hold in Italy. Many traditional cheeses disappeared, but others were improved and became more widespread as a result of scientific research and more efficient production systems. Cheesemakers had a greater understanding of the importance of temperature and humidity control, as well as the importance of hygiene.

At the end of the 1980s it was estimated that more than 400 different types of cheese were being produced in Italy. In this book we have tried to identify and describe the better-known and most widely available types. Even so, the choice was arduous, and the exclusion of many remarkable cheeses is due entirely to lack of space rather than regard.

The production of many cheeses is controlled by government regulations that guarantee quality and protect regional varieties from poorer imitations. Beginning in 1955 some cheeses became DOC (*Denominazione di Origine Controllata*). In 1995 a new DOP (*Denominazione di Origine Protetta*) category was introduced. The cheeses listed below are all DOP.

C = cow's
G = goat's
E = ewe's
WB = water buffalo's

Type of Cheese	Province of Production	Milk
Asiago	Padova, Trento, Treviso, Vicenza	C
Bitto	Sondrio, Bergamo	C - C/G
Bra	Cuneo, Turin	C - C/G/E
Caciocavallo Silano	Crotone, Catanzaro, Cosenza, Avellino, Benevento, Caserta, Naples, Isernia, Campobasso, Bari, Taranto, Brindisi, Matera, Potenza	C
Canestrato Pugliese	Foggia	E
Casciotta d'Urbino	Pesaro	E/C
Castelmagno	Cuneo	C -C/G/E
Fiore Sardo	Cagliari, Nuoro, Oristano, Sassari	E
Fontina	Aosta	C
Formai de Mut dell'Alta Val Brembana	Bergamo	C
Gorgonzola	Cuneo, Novara, Vercelli, Bergamo, Brescia, Como, Cremona, Lodi, Milan, Pavia	C
Grana Padano	Lodi, Bergamo, Brescia, Como, Cremona, Mantua, Milan, Pavia, Sondrio, Varese, Alessandria, Asti, Cuneo, Novara, Turin, Vercelli, Trento, Padua, Rovigo, Treviso, Venice, Verona, Vicenza, Bologna, Ferrara, Forlì, Piacenza, Ravenna	C
Montasio	Udine, Pordenone, Gorizia, Trieste, Belluno, Treviso, Padua, Venice	C
Monte Veronese	Verona	C
Mozzarella di Bufala Campana	Caserta, Salerno, Frosinone, Latina, Naples, Benevento, Rome	WB
Murazzano	Cuneo	E - E/C
Parmigiano Reggiano	Modena, Parma, Reggio, Emilia, Mantua, Bologna	C
Pecorino Romano	Rome, Rieti, Viterbo, Latina, Grosseto, Cagliari, Nuoro, Oristano, Sassari	E
Pecorino Sardo	Cagliari, Nuoro, Oristano, Sassari	E
Pecorino Siciliano	Catania, Enna, Trapani, Caltanissetta, Palermo, Ragusa, Siracusa, Messina, Agrigento	E
Pecorino Toscano	Arezzo, Pisa, Massa, Carrara, Livorno, Grosseto, Florence, Prato, Lucca, Pistoia, Siena, Terni, Perugia, Viterbo	E
Provolone Valpadana	Brescia, Cremona, Padova, Piacenza, Rovigo, Verona, Vicenza, Bergamo, Mantua, Milan, Trento	C
Quartirolo Lombardo	Bergamo, Brescia, Como, Cremona, Lodi, Milan, Pavia, Varese	C
Ragusano	Ragusa, Siracusa	C
Raschera	Cuneo	C - C/E/G
Robiola di Roccaverano	Alessandria, Asti	C/E/G
Taleggio	Bergamo, Brescia, Como, Cremona, Lodi, Milano, Pavia, Treviso, Novara	C
Toma Piemontese	Alessandria, Asti, Biella, Cuneo, Novara, Turin, Vercelli,	C
Valle d'Aosta Fromadzo	Aosta	C - C/E - G
Valtellina Casera	Sondrio	C

Making Cheese

Above: Some of the best cheeses in Italy are made in the northern alpine regions. This farmer from Piedmont is holding a local variety of Toma.

Below and center page: Parmesan cheese is made by curdling milk which is partially skimmed half way through the coagulating process. Whey from an earlier batch is then added. More than 1,000 lb (500 kg) of cow's milk is required to make just one form (wheel) of Parmesan.

Cheese is made of curd, a semisolid substance that forms when milk coagulates, or curdles. Milk curdles naturally if left at room temperature for long enough, and in some areas of the world fresh cheese is made in this way. In Italy, thousands of years of cheesemaking has refined this process and an estimated 400 types of cheeses are produced. Almost all are made in the same way; by solidifying milk, adding salt, and evaporating part of the whey (the watery liquid that separates from the curds). For hard cheeses, the curds must then be cooked in order to completely evaporate the whey and create a better consistency. The cheese is then poured into molds called *fascere* and left to dry. The aging process completes the cheese, and can last for months or even years in the *casere*, or cheese warehouses. There the cheeses are repeatedly turned, in order to maintain a consistent texture.

The fat content in cheese must be evaluated in comparison with its dry weight. A "high fat" cheese has more than 42% fat. If the fat content is between 20–42% it is called a "semi-fat" cheese, and if less than 20% it is classified as "low fat."

Depending on the production process, cheese is divided into two categories:

Soft cheeses – with more than 40% water content.
Hard cheeses – with less than 40% water content.

Left: Forms of Ricotta and Pecorino are left to dry in Lazio.

Soft cheeses are further divided into three categories: fresh, aged, and fermented. Hard cheeses are categorized as: raw, cooked, and fermented.

Italian cheeses are divided in two general categories: table cheese and grating cheese. Table cheeses are served at the end of the meal, but before dessert and fruit. They should be accompanied by foods that enhance their taste, texture, and aroma. Cooked cheeses go well with grapes and strawberries. Olives complement raw and hard cheeses, and Pecorino cheeses are excellent with fava beans (broad beans), or pears.

Above: Fontina cheese is aged in underground caves where the rind is salted every day for three months.

Below: Shepherd with his flock in the Alps in Valle d'Aosta.

Cheese and Wine

Above: Grapes ripen on the vine in the gathering dusk. Italy has even more varieties of wine than it does cheese.

Below: Combining food and wine to show them both to their best advantage is an art. However, don't be put off or overawed by the task. With Italian foods, a good rule of thumb is to serve regional foods with wines from the same areas. You can generally assume that the locals will have perfected the art of combining the two over many centuries.

In Italian Renaissance courts, among those assigned to the kitchens was a *maestro di taglio*, or "specialist of the blade." His job was to cut and arrange different types of cheese, according to precise rules. Preparing cheese for the courtly table was a ritual and a specialized art. Today, for formal occasions, or even a casual meal, certain rules and criteria regarding the foods and wines which best complement cheeses should be followed.

A cheese board should contain a wide selection of flavors and types of cheese. The minimum assortment should offer at least six different cheeses: three mild soft varieties (one from each type of milk: cow's, goat's, and ewe's), plus a flavorful soft cheese, a pressed cheese, and a herb cheese. The cheese board should be served with a selection of fruit, vegetables, preserves, and wine to enhance the cheeses' different aromas, tastes, and textures.

Fresh Cheeses

Fresh cheeses should be coupled with wines that do not mask their delicate flavor, such as light white wines or fresh, fruity rosés. If served with fresh apricots, cherries, strawberries, raspberries, grapes, or candied fruit, they are best with Moscato and Sauterne dessert wines.

High Fat Cheeses

High fat cheeses require wines that accentuate the buttery part of the cheese and enhance the flavor, such as spicy white wines or decisive reds. Green tomatoes (such as Mexican tomatillos), with their strong taste and sweet-and-sour flavor, are perfect for eating with these types of cheeses.

Delicate Soft Cheeses

Soft, delicate cheeses go well with light, aromatic white wines, and soft reds. They are delicious when served with strawberries, grapes, almonds, candied fruits, and honey.

Flavorful Soft Cheeses

Flavorful soft cheeses are best with robust and smooth red wines, but also with dry, full-flavored white wines. Plums, fresh prunes, and chestnut honey will enhance the taste and aroma of these cheeses.

Sharp and Piquant Cheeses

Dry red wines, strawberry jam, and acacia honey – slightly liquid and sweet – are great accompaniments to these types of cheeses.

Hard Aged Cheeses

Aged cheese should be paired with dry, full-bodied red wines and can also be served with persimmons (sharon fruit), pears, and fresh peaches. Orange-flower honey, with its delicate citrus flavor, is a perfect match for these cheeses.

Herb Cheeses

Herb cheeses have a savory and decisive flavor and go well with white dessert wines, such as Sauterne, Port, or Malvasia. They should be served with grapes, walnuts, and celery.

Caprini

Caprini (goat's) cheese can be served with either white or red wines which are light and fresh.

Above: Parmesan is a noble cheese; a good book, a glass of wine, and a slice of aged Parmesan – what more could you ask for?

Below: Many cheeses go very well with fresh or dried fruit.

Asiago

This cheese originally comes from the Asiago plateau, which nestles in among the towering Dolomite Mountains in the Veneto region of northern Italy. It is now also made in some neighboring provinces, as well as in the Trentino region to the north. It represents about one fourth of the total cheese production in the Veneto region. There are now two quite distinct types of Asiago: *d'allevo* and *pressato*. The aged varieties of *d'allevo* have a sharp, pungent flavor, and, confusingly, the locals sometimes refer to them as Pecorino (sheep's cheese), which is often strong-tasting.

ASIAGO

MAIN PRODUCTION ZONES: *Veneto (Vicenza, Padua, Treviso) and Trentino (Trento)*

MADE FROM: *cow's milk*

SEASON: *year round*

Asiago d'allevo *(for the table or grating)*
AGING: *4 months to 2 years*
FAT: *34%*
TASTE: *sharp*

Asiago pressato *(for the table)*
AGING: *20–40 days*
FAT: *44%*
TASTE: *almost sweet, buttery*

Green Beans with Asiago
(Serves 4)

Ingredients
- 1 onion, finely chopped
- 1 clove garlic, finely chopped
- 3½ tbsp butter
- 2 tbsp extra-virgin olive oil
- 12 oz/350 g green/French beans
- salt and and freshly ground black pepper
- 10 oz/300 g Asiago cheese, cut into strips

Sauté the onion and garlic in the butter and oil. Add the green beans, salt, and pepper, cover, and cook over low heat for about 10 minutes. If necessary, add a few tablespoons of water. When the green beans are tender, add the cheese. Cover and cook until the cheese has melted.

Wine: a full-bodied, dry red (Amarone Quintarelli)

Asiago pressato

Asiago pressato is produced in wheels that are about 12–16 in (30–40 cm) in diameter and 4–6 in (10–15 cm) in height. Each form weighs from 18–26 lb (8–12 kg.) It is made with full cream cow's milk and has quite a high fat content. Asiago pressato is the best known of the two types and represents about 75 percent of all Asiago made. It is an excellent table cheese.

Asiago pressato is pale gold with a reddish-yellow exterior.

Color varies from white to pale gold. Pitted texture dotted with small, irregularly placed holes.

The Asiago trade mark. This is stamped into the crust of the forms. Asiago is a D.O.C. cheese (see Introduction).

Asiago d'allevo has a smooth exterior, ranging in color from straw to medium brown, depending on age.

Grainy texture, pitted with holes (smaller than the younger pressato variety). Deeper color.

Asiago d'allevo

The forms of Asiago *d'allevo* are just slightly smaller than the *pressato* type. Depending on its age, Asiago d'allevo is known at 6 months as *Mezzano*, at 1 year as *Vecchio*, and at 2 years as *Stravecchio*. The more it is aged, the sharper its taste becomes.

Bagoss

agoss takes its name from the local dialect term for "from the town of Bagolino," which is a well known cheese-producing town in Lombardy. According to local legend, Bagoss was one of the favorite cheeses of the Risorgimento hero, Giuseppe Garibaldi (who helped to unite Italy). Bagoss is both an excellent table cheese and good for grating. It can also be used for cooking. In one traditional recipe from Lombardy, slabs of Bagoss are grilled and then served over polenta.

BAGOSS

MAIN PRODUCTION ZONES: Lombardy (Bagolino)

AGING: 1–4 years

MADE FROM: skimmed cow's milk

FAT: 30%

SEASON: summer

TASTE: rich, fruity, robust but not spicy

The cheese that sighs

Wheels of Bagoss are about 16 in (40 cm) in diameter and 5 in (13 cm) in height. Bagoss has a special, almost fruity flavor. It is sometimes called the "cheese that sighs" because when the aged forms are cut they release air in a rush that sounds like a human sigh. Bagoss is also called *Grana bresciano* for its rich and robust flavor.

Thick, dark brown crust develops to protect cheese after brushing with flax oil.

Warm yellow color, given by the saffron in the mixture. Grainy texture.

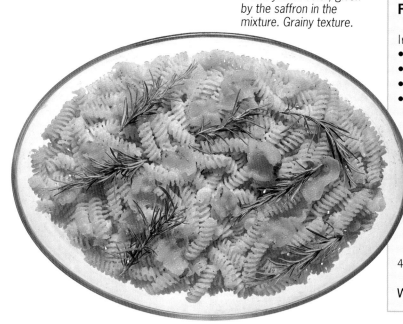

Fusilli with Bagoss (Serves 4)

Ingredients
- 14 oz/450 g fusilli pasta
- 4 oz/125 g grated Bagoss cheese
- 2 tbsp heavy/double cream
- salt and freshly ground black pepper
- 8 thin slices of pancetta or bacon
- 8–10 sprigs fresh rosemary

Cook the pasta in plenty of boiling, salted water until *al dente*. Drain and return to the pan. Add the cheese and cream and season with salt and pepper. Set aside to rest for 2–3 minutes. Line an ovenproof baking dish with the pork fat and scatter with the rosemary. Cover with the pasta and bake in a preheated oven at 450°F/230°C/gas 7 for 10 minutes. Serve hot.

Wine: a dry red (Pinot Nero)

Bitto

Bitto is made in just a few mountain valleys in the Valtellina area of Lombardy. It is quite rare, and much sought after by gourmet chefs. It origins are lost in the mists of time, although the locals claim that they were taught the art of cheesemaking by the Celts when the ancient Romans forced them into their mountain valleys. They say the name derives from the Celtic term "bitu," which means "eternity." More prosaically, it was probably named after the Bitto River which flows through the region.

Shape and aging

Bitto wheels vary greatly in size and weight. The largest weigh about 55 lb (25 kg). Cheesemakers in the tiny production area carry the forms high into the mountains each spring so that the cheese is not affected by the summer heat. Traditionally, a small amount (maximum 10%) of goat's milk was added to the cheese.

VALTELLINA
Bergamo · Sondrio
LOMBARDY

BITTO

PRODUCTION ZONE: *Lombardy (Sondrio, Bergamasco)*

AGING: *70 days to 3 years, exceptionally, up to 10 years*

MADE FROM: *whole cow's milk*

FAT: *45%*

SEASON: *summer*

TASTE: *sweet and aromatic when young, sharp and robust when aged*

Aged Bitto is firm and flaky, yet maintains a softness. Younger Bitto is soft and white in color.

Bitto Fritters
(Serves 4)

Ingredients
- 1 cup/150 g all-purpose/plain flour
- 1 cup/150 g rye flour
- 1 tsp salt
- about ½ cup/125 ml lukewarm water
- 8 oz/250 g Bitto cheese, thinly sliced
- 1 tsp grappa
- 4 oz/125 g pork fat/lard for frying

In a large bowl, mix the two types of flour with the salt and enough water to make a dense batter. Set aside to rest for 1 hour. Stir the cheese and grappa into the batter. Heat the pork fat in a large skillet (frying pan) to very hot. Place 2 tablespoons of the cheese and batter in the skillet for each fritter. Turn to cook on both sides. Drain on paper towels. Repeat until the batter is finished. Serve the fritters piping hot.

Wine: a full-bodied, dry red (Franciacorta Rosso)

Bra

Bra is made in many areas of Piedmont, but takes its name from the small town which has always been its major marketplace. There are quite strict rules governing its manufacture; for example, cow's that produce the milk to make it must only be fed on fresh grass or hay. It is the third most-produced cheese in Piedmont, after Toma and Fontina. There are two types, *duro* (firm) and *tenero* (soft). Bra is particularly sought after in the neighboring region of Liguria, where it is used to produce a tasty pesto (basil sauce).

Alpine Bra

The alpine variety of Bra is produced in mountain villages. The forms are cylindrical, 12–16 in (30–40 cm) in diameter and usually weigh less than 18 lb (8 kg). The soft variety is a whitish ivory color with a gray outer crust. The firm variety, which is aged for longer, becomes a straw color with a yellow, or ocher colored outer shell.

BRA

Main production zones: Piedmont (province of Cuneo)

Aging: from 45 days (soft) to 6 months (firm)

Made from: cow's milk

Fat: 32%

Season: year round

Taste: soft Bra is delicate and aromatic, firm Bra is sharp and salty.

Firm Bra is sharp and salty, with a straw color.

Soft Bra has a light grey crust.

Bra Fondue
(Serves 6)

Ingredients
- 1 lb/500 g Bra cheese, diced
- 1 cup/250 ml full cream milk
- 1 cup/250 ml heavy/double cream
- salt to taste
- day-old bread, diced

Let the cheese rest in the milk for 2–3 hours. Transfer the cheese and milk to a fondue pot and place it in another pan filled with boiling water. Add the cream and salt, and mix well. Remove the fondue pot from the larger pan of water and place it over the flame on its fondue stand in the center of the table. Do not let the fondue boil. Arrange the diced bread on a platter. Each diner uses their fondue fork to dip dices of bread into the fondue.

Wine: a dry red (Barbera)

Caciocavallo

Caciocavallo is produced in the regions that once belonged to the Kingdom of Naples. It has been produced there since medieval times. Today, it is easily the most popular and widely used cheese in southern Italy. Its shape, reminiscent of a pear "with a noose around its neck," is created by the cord used to hang the cheese during the aging or smoking processes. Its name (literally: "horse-cheese") is said to be derived from the way the forms of caciocavallo are tied in pairs one each end of a cord and hung from a beam or hook so that they look like a rider's legs dangling from a horse.

CACIOCAVALLO

PRODUCTION ZONE: Calabria, Lucania, Puglia, Campania, and Sicily
AGING: 90 days to 2 years
MADE FROM: cow's milk
Fat: 44%
Season: year round
TASTE: from delicately sweet to sharp, depending on age.

A cord is used to hang the cheese during the aging or smoking processes, creating Caciocavallo's distinctive pear shape.

Serving Caciocavallo

Young Caciocavallo makes an excellent table cheese, while the older cheese is good both for the table and for grating. Caciocavallo is an ideal cooking cheese, because it melts quickly and uniformly. The forms vary greatly in size, although an average form will weigh about 4 lb (2 kg). The cheese itself varies from white to creamy yellow and is compact, elastic, and firm when sliced. Aged Caciocavallo is harder and more flaky.

Creamy yellow color inside.

Smooth crust.

The color of the crust varies from cream to yellow and brown.

Caciocavallo podolico

This very rare cheese is made from the milk of Podolica cows which are an ancient, semi-wild southern Italian breed that feed on the local grasses and herbs. Special care is taken in aging the cheese, which is light brown in color. Caciocavallo podolico is almost impossible to find in even southern Italy; don't expect to find it in your local supermarket!

Baked Vegetables with Caciocavallo
(Serves 4)

Ingredients
- 1 eggplant/aubergine, thinly sliced
- 2 large potatoes, thinly sliced
- 2 large carrots, thinly sliced
- 2 large zucchini/courgettes, thinly sliced
- 1 bell pepper/capsicum, cut in strips
- 2 bunches of radicchio, shredded
- 4 tbsp extra-virgin olive oil
- salt and freshly ground black pepper to taste
- 2 tbsp finely chopped fresh oregano
- 4 oz/125 g Caciocavallo cheese, sliced

Place the prepared vegetables in an oiled ovenproof baking dish. Drizzle with the oil, and sprinkle with salt, pepper, and oregano. Bake in a preheated oven at 400°F/200°C/gas 6 for about 20 minutes. Cover the vegetables with slices of cheese and return the dish to the oven for 5–10 minutes, or until the cheese melts.

Wine: a dry rosé (Salice Salentino Rosato)

Caciocavallo is an ideal table cheese, but also perfect for use in cooking, as it melts smoothly and evenly.

Caciocavallo is mentioned in a novella written by the Florentine author Franco Sacchetti in the 14th century. This suggests that the cheese was already known well beyond the limits of its production zone.

Caciotta

The term "Caciotta" is a generic name for a variety of cheeses made by small producers in central Italy. It derives from the Latin *caseus* (cheese). Caciotta cheeses can be quite different from each other, depending on the region in which they are produced. Some are aged in walnut leaves, others are flavored with peppercorns or other spices, including chili pepper. Caciotta is normally consumed fresh or only slightly aged. The few that are aged are good for grating.

Thin, smooth, light-colored crust.

CACIOTTA

PRODUCTION ZONE: central Italy (Tuscany, Umbria, the Marches, Lazio)

AGING: varies according to the area in which it is produced

MADE FROM: ewe's milk, or a mixture of ewe's and cow's milk

FAT: varies

SEASON: year round

TASTE: sweet and delicate

Forms

The forms (wheels) are usually quite small, weighing about 2 lb/1 kg. The interior is firm, soft, and white with few air holes. Made in small quantities by traditional cheesemakers, the quality is normally excellent.

19

Whole-Wheat Rigatoni with Caciotta
(Serves 4)

Ingredients
- 12 oz/350 g whole-wheat/wholemeal rigatoni pasta
- 2 potatoes, diced
- 4 oz/125 g Caciotta cheese
- 1/2 cup/125 ml full cream milk
- 4 tbsp butter
- salt and freshly ground black pepper to taste
- 3/4 cup/60 g freshly grated Parmesan cheese

Cook the rigatoni and potatoes in a large pan of boiling, salted water. Place the Caciotta, milk, and butter in the top of a double boiler and cook until the cheese is melted. Season with salt and pepper. Drain the pasta and potatoes when the pasta is cooked *al dente*. Pour the cheese sauce over the pasta, sprinkle with the Parmesan, mix well, and serve.

Wine: a dry red (Chianti Classico)

Canestrato Pugliese

Canestrato owes its name to the traditional cheesemaking technique of Puglia, in which wicker baskets are used to shape and set the cheeses. Canestrato has been produced this way for centuries; the method still in use today is described in Homer's epic poem the *Odyssey*, which dates to before the 8th century BC! This cheese is made almost exclusively from the milk of ewes that have been pasture fed, and not milked more than twice a day.

Crust clearly marked with indentations from the baskets in which it sets.

"Canestro" or basket, from which the cheese obtains its distinctive marking and shape.

Making Canestrato

After the coagulation of the curds, the forms of cheese are placed in individual baskets which give them their typically wrinkled, patterned outer layer. The cheese is then salted, either by the classic method of spreading salt over the outer layer, or by immersing the entire round in brine. Nowadays, the herds from the high pastures of Puglia are also kept in the low pastures of Abruzzi, and the production of Canestrato Pugliese has spread throughout southern Italy.

Penne with Olives and Canestrato

(Serves 4)

Ingredients
- ½ cup/125 g butter
- ½ cup/75 g flour
- 2 cups/500 ml milk
- salt and freshly ground pepper
- pinch of nutmeg
- 1 lb/500 g penne pasta
- 4 tbsp bread crumbs
- 10 oz/300 g aged Canestrato Pugliese cheese, cubed
- 1 cup/100 g black olives, pitted and chopped

Prepare a bechamel sauce: melt half the butter and add the flour, stirring continuously with a wooden spoon. Add the milk and cook until it becomes dense, stirring continuously to keep it smooth. Add salt, pepper, and nutmeg to taste. Cook the pasta in a large pan of salted, boiling water until *al dente*. Drain well. Butter an ovenproof baking dish, and sprinkle with half the bread crumbs. Combine the pasta with the bechamel sauce, adding the cheese and olives. Mix well, then transfer to the baking dish. Sprinkle with the remaining butter and bread crumbs. Bake in a preheated oven at 350°F/180°C/gas 4 for 15–20 minutes, or until golden brown. Serve hot.

Wine: a dry red (Cirò Rosso)

Crust varies in color from yellow to brown, depending on age.

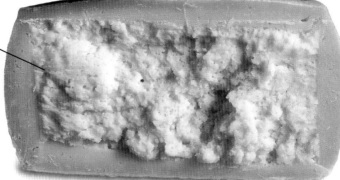

Compact and flaky texture.

The aging process
The Canestrato is first placed in wicker baskets to set. It is then removed and placed over wild fennel stems, which enhance the flavor.

The sharp flavor of Canestrato is perfectly complemented by black olives.

Caprino

Classic Caprino is made exclusively from whole or partially skimmed goat's milk, hence the name (*capra* means "goat" in Italian). Nowadays, most commercially produced Caprino is made from cow's milk. Caprino is generally served fresh in salads, or with spices and aromatic herbs. It is also used to flavor sauces. Aged Caprino is generally saltier. The two most well-known types of caprino come from Roccaverano, where they are wrapped in walnut leaves, and Sardinia, which are quite spicy.

CAPRINO

PRODUCTION ZONE: originally from the Como area, but today throughout Italy

AGING: none for fresh Caprino, 20–40 days for aged Caprino

MADE FROM: authentic Caprino – goat's milk; industrially produced Caprino – cow's milk

SEASON: varies

FAT: year round

TASTE: delicate with a slight tang for fresh Caprino; slightly sharper acid tang for aged Caprino

Wild salad greens are very popular in Italy. They are gathered in the fields and sold in select vegetable stores and markets. You can replace them by combining several types of radicchio, endives/chicory, rocket, and escarole/curly endive.

Wild Salad Greens with Warm Caprino
(Serves 2)

Ingredients
- mixed wild salad greens, well washed and thoroughly dried
- 3 tbsp extra-virgin olive oil
- ½ cup/60 g pitted black olives
- 1 tbsp honey
- salt to taste
- 4 small forms Caprino cheese

Divide the salad greens among two serving plates. In a blender, chop the olives with 2 tablespoons of oil and the honey until creamy. Season the individual salads with salt and drizzle with the remaining olive oil. Heat the cheese in a preheated oven at 350°F/180°C/gas 4 for 5-10 minutes. Place two Caprini on top of each salad. Drizzle or spoon the olive cream over the top.

Wine: a light, dry white (Tocai Colli Orientali)

Caprino stagionato

Aged Caprini ("Caprini" is the plural form of "Caprino") come in small round or squarish shapes. The outer layer is yellowish and quite thin. Depending on the age, the cheese itself varies from soft to creamy to compact. Some smoked Caprini are also made.

Fresh Caprino covered in herbs for aging.

Caprino shrinks as it ages, and the crust colors and thickens.

Caprino preserved in oil

Since fresh Caprini should be eaten within a week or two of being made, they are not widely available outside of Italy. However, they are available in bottled form, preserved in olive oil, usually with the addition of herbs and spices.

The bottled Caprino is often in the shape of bocconcini, or bite-sized pieces.

Dried chili pepper is often added to the bottled Caprini. For a little extra "zing," pour a little of the oil over the cheese when serving.

Caprino fresco

Fresh Caprino comes in round or cylindrical shapes. It has no crust or outer layer and is generally wrapped in paper. The cheese is very soft and creamy. While the cow's milk (or mixed goat's and cow's milk) varieties are often delicious, do try the authentic goat's milk type. Serve it with fresh green salad and just a touch of extra-virgin olive oil. It really is divine!

Crescenza and other Fresh Cheeses

Crescenza is an ancient cheese, made in Lombardy long before fresh cheeses became as fashionable as they are today. Its name comes from the Latin *crescere*, meaning to grow, because of the peculiar way in which the cheese ferments and inflates. Stracchino, Raveggiolo, and Squaquarone are all similar cheeses. Originally, they were produced in the fall when the cattle herds returned from the alpine pastures where they spent the summer. Nowadays Crescenza and Stracchino are produced almost purely on an industrial basis and are available all over Italy in a variety of types, all more or less creamy and flavorful.

LOMBARDY
EMILIA-ROMAGNA
TUSCANY

CRESCENZA/STRACCHINO

MAIN PRODUCTION ZONES: Lombardy
AGING: 5–6 days
MADE FROM: whole, pasteurized cow's milk
FAT: 48%
SEASON: year round
TASTE: sweet, delicate, and buttery

SQUAQUARONE

MAIN PRODUCTION ZONES: Emilia-Romagna
Otherwise the same as Crescenza and Stracchino

RAVEGGIOLO

MAIN PRODUCTION ZONES: Emilia-Romagna and Tuscany (Apennine region)
FAT: 45%
Otherwise the same as Crescenza and Stracchino

The texture of Crescenza is soft and it is milky white in color.

Crescenza

Crescenza usually comes in small squares or rectangles about 8 in (20 cm) long. Soft and spreadable, it is milky white in color. Originally Crescenza and Stracchino were produced and stored in different ways, but the new industrially produced varieties are almost identical. Crescenza goes very well with white wine, and also with beer.

Raveggiolo comes in small round or rectangular forms.

Raveggiolo

Raveggiolo is a soft cream cheese with no outer layer. It is white and very smooth and creamy. It originated in the Apennines between Emilia-Romagna and Tuscany. At first it was made with a mixture of ewe's and cow's milk, but is now made exclusively with cow's milk.

Squaquarone

Squaquarone is so fresh and creamy that it can not hold any particular shape. It often releases liquid, hence the name which derives from the dialect term "*squacquerarsi*" (to lose water). It has a sweet and delicate flavor and is normally served with focaccia or piadine.

Stracchino is soft, white and spreadable.

Stracchino

Stracchino used to be a fairly generic term for a number of quite different cheeses, but nowadays it refers almost exclusively to a Crescenza-like fresh cheese. It always has a very thin, soft, and completely edible skin. A skimmed variety of Stracchino, made from low fat milk also exists. In the region of Lombardy, at Christmas time, it is a tradition to eat this type of Stracchino accompanied by the famous "Mostarda" (candied fruit in a syrup containing white mustard), a specialty of Cremona.

Piadina with Squaquarone

(Serves 4–6)

Ingredients
- 5 cups/750 g flour
- ³⁄₄ cup/225 g shortening or lard
- ¹⁄₂ tsp active dried yeast
- 1 tsp salt
- 1¹⁄₂ cups/450 ml lukewarm water
- 2 tbsp extra-virgin olive oil
- 8 oz/250 g Squaquarone cheese

Heap the flour up on a work surface and make a well in the center. Melt the shortening or lard in a double boiler and pour it into the well. Dissolve the yeast and salt in the water. Gradually pour the liquid into the well and mix it in with your hands to make a dough. Knead the dough until smooth and elastic, adding the oil a little at a time as you knead. Divide the dough into 9 pieces. Shape each piece into a ball. Roll out each piece of dough to about 6-7 in/15-18 cm in diameter. Cook the dough on a cast iron or terra-cotta griddle. When cooked, spread the cheese onto the middle of each piadina. Fold in half and warm again on the griddle.

Wine: a dry red (Sangiovese di Romagna)

Fiore Sardo

Fiore Sardo is one of the best of the many Pecorino (ewe's milk) cheeses produced in Sardinia. Some say that the name derives from the now extinct practice of using the extract of wild flowers to make the curds. The name was already in use in the 18th century, although the origins of this cheese are certainly much older. Fiore Sardo is made according to strict government regulations. The milk must come only from Sardinian sheep (a breed that is thought to descend from the mouflon), and the cheese must be produced on the island itself.

FIORE SARDO

MAIN PRODUCTION ZONES: Sardinia
AGING: 3-6 months
MADE FROM: Ewe's milk
FAT: 45%
SEASON: year round
TASTE: full, decisive and slightly sharp

SARDINIA

Bright yellow to dark brown crust, made by rubbing with olive oil and sheep fat during aging.

Firm texture, white to pale yellow in color. Aged varieties crumbly.

Aging and uses

Some forms, especially those destined to be aged, are lightly smoked (you can recognize them by their black crusts). Aged Fiore Sardo is ideal for grating. Traditionally it is the best cheese to use when making a real Genoese pesto (basil sauce for pasta).

Crêpes with Fiore Sardo
(Serves 2–3)

Ingredients
- 6 eggs
- 1/2 cup/125 ml milk
- 5 tbsp flour
- salt and freshly ground black pepper to taste
- 1/3 cup/90 g butter
- 4 oz/125 g Fiore Sardo cheese, shavings
- 6 sage leaves

Beat the eggs in a bowl with a whisk. Add the milk, then gradually stir in the flour, salt, and pepper to make a smooth batter. Grease a crêpe pan with a little butter and pour in one-sixth of the batter. Flip the crêpe when light golden brown on one side and brown on the other. Repeat until all the batter is used up. Cover each crêpe with cheese and roll it very loosely. Arrange the crêpes in an ovenproof baking dish. Melt the remaining butter and pour over the top. Sprinkle with the sage and bake in a preheated oven at 350°F/180°C/gas 4 for about 10 minutes. Serve hot.

Wine: a dry, fruity white (Alghero Bianco)

Fontina

Fontina cheese has been made for at least 500 years. Its production was meticulously described in medieval times. The origin of the name is controversial. It may derive from the Fontin Mountains, or the village of Fontinaz, or from the way it melts (*fondere*, in Italian). Production is strictly controlled, and the milk used must come from a special breed of Valle d'Aosta cows, known for the high quality and rich flavor of their milk.

VALLE D'AOSTA

FONTINA

MAIN PRODUCTION ZONES: Valle d'Aosta
AGING: 3 months
MADE FROM: unpasteurized, whole cow's milk
FAT: 45%
SEASON: year round
TASTE: sweet, very distinctive, full flavor

Baked Gnocchi with Fontina
(Serves 4)

Ingredients
- 2 lb/1 kg potatoes, boiled
- 1 tsp salt
- 2 cups/300 g all-purpose/plain flour
- 1 egg
- 3 oz/90 g Fontina cheese, sliced
- 3 tbsp freshly grated Parmesan cheese
- 3½ tbsp butter
- ⅔ cup/150 ml milk

Mash the potatoes. Fold in the salt, flour, and egg and mix well. On a floured work surface, roll the mixture into cylinders about ¾ in/ 2 cm thick. Cut them into pieces about 1 in/ 2.5 cm long. Cook the gnocchi in 2 or 3 batches in a large pan of salted, boiling, water. When they bob up to the surface cook for 2–3 minutes more. Remove with a slotted spoon, drain well, and transfer to a buttered ovenproof baking dish. Cover with the Fontina, Parmesan, and dabs of butter. Pour the milk over the top and cook in the oven at 400°F/200°C/gas 6 for 5 minutes, or until nicely browned.

Wine: a dry red (Nebbiolo d'Alba)

Appearance and uses
Wheels of Fontina are about 16 in (40 cm) in diameter and 3 in (8 cm) tall. They weigh about 18–40 lb (8–18 kg) Fontina has a delicious nutty flavor and makes a perfect table cheese. Because it melts so beautifully, it is also excellent for cooking. The traditional Valle d'Aosta *Fonduta* (fondue) is made using Fontina.

Thin, orange-gold crust.

Soft, elastic, buttery texture, with pungent aroma.

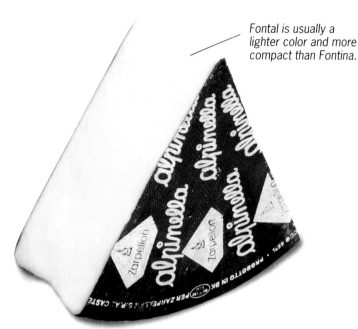

Fontal is usually a lighter color and more compact than Fontina.

Fontal

Fontina's fame has spawned a host of similar cheeses, most of which are produced in northern Italy. They can be found in stores as Fontal. They are similar to Fontina, but lack the authentic cheese's special flavor, and cost slightly less.

Leek and Fontal Country Pie
(Serves 8)

Ingredients:
For the pie crust:
- 1 cup/150 g all-purpose/plain flour
- 1 tsp salt
- 4 tbsp extra-virgin olive oil
- about ½ cup/125 ml cold water
Filling:
- 2 lb/1 kg leeks, thinly sliced
- 2 tbsp extra-virgin olive oil
- salt and freshly ground black pepper to taste
- 2 eggs + 1 extra egg yolk
- 10 oz/300 g Fontal cheese, diced
- 2 tbsp finely chopped parsley

Pie crust: Sift the flour and salt into a mixing bowl. Add the olive oil and a small amount of cold water (a spoonful at a time) and mix until combined. Knead until smooth and elastic. Wrap in plastic wrap (cling film) and chill in the refrigerator for 20 minutes.

Filling: Sauté the leeks in the oil until soft. Season with salt and pepper. Cook until the leeks are done. In a large bowl, beat the 2 whole eggs and add the Fontal and parsley. Finally, add the sauteéd leeks to the egg mixture.

On a floured work surface, roll out two-thirds of the pie dough with a rolling pin. Use it to line a 12 in/30 cm diameter oiled pie pan (dish). Fill with the leek and egg mixture. Roll out the remaining dough and cut into strips. Place them across the filling like the spokes of a wheel. Brush with an egg wash made from the remaining egg yolk mixed with a little water. Bake at 375°F/190°C/gas 5 for 30 minutes, then lower the temperature and bake for an additional 15 minutes. Serve hot or warm.

Wine: a dry red (Donnaz)

Gorgonzola

Gorgonzola takes its name from a locality in Lombardy, near Milan, where it has been made for centuries. According to legend, this cheese was invented by accident when a love-sick cheesemaker, late for an amorous rendez-vous, left some curds out overnight. The following morning, hoping to cover up his mistake, he mixed them in with the rest. To his horror, when the cheese was opened several months later it was veined with greeny-blue mold. All was forgiven on tasting the moldy brew which was found to be delicious. Gorgonzola is now made in two versions — *dolce* and *piccante*.

GORGONZOLA

MAIN PRODUCTION ZONES: Piedmont, particularly around Novara, and to a lesser extent, Lombardy.

AGING: 2 months (dolce), 3 months (piccante).

MADE FROM: pasteurized cow's milk.

FAT: 48%.

SEASON: year round

TASTE: creamy, pleasantly sharp (dolce), sharp and tangy (piccante).

The sweet creamy taste of Gorgonzola dolce teams up nicely with many raw fruits and vegetables.

Serve the celery stalks stuffed with Gorgonzola dolce with their leafy tops for a natural and colorful look.

Gorgonzola Dolce with Celery
(Serves 4)

Ingredients
- 2 oz/60 g Gorgonzola dolce
- 8 stalks celery

Clean the stalks of celery, removing any tough fibers. Wash thoroughly and dry. Fill the stalks with the Gorgonzola dolce (kept at room temperature for 1–2 hours).

Wine: a dry, sparkling white (Prosecco)

Gorgonzola Piccante with Grannysmith Apples
(Serves 4)

Ingredients
- 2 Grannysmith apples
- juice of 1 lemon
- 2 oz/60 g Gorgonzola piccante

Wash the apples. Core them and cut each one into about 12 slices. Drizzle with the lemon juice, then arrange on a serving dish. Cover with slices of Gorgonzola piccante.

Tronchetto

In Tronchetto, the creamy tang of Gorgonzola dolce is alternated with layers of delicately flavored Mascarpone cheese. Authentic Mascarpone goes off very quickly, so this mixture should be consumed within a day or two of production.

Layers of Gorgonzola dolce.

Layers of Mascarpone.

Gorgonzola Dolce

Gorgonzola dolce is made of pasteurized cow's milk. It is produced throughout the year and aged for two months. During the aging process, the forms of cheese are continually pierced with long thick needles to promote the growth of the characteristic blue-green mold. Gorgonzola dolce is a marketing success story in Italy where, since the end of the war, it has gone from being yet another local northern cheese, to a national bestseller.

Soft, spreadable texture with colors ranging from white to light creamy yellow, and veined with blue-green penicillium glaucum *mold.*

Gorgonzola Piccante

Although 90 percent of the Gorgonzola produced in Italy today is *dolce*, the *piccante* (spicy) variety has a blend of merits all its own. Aged in the same way as the *dolce*, with only a slightly longer period of heating, Gorgonzola piccante has a sharp, slightly acid taste which is particularly good served spread with honey or any of the sweet northern Italian fruit mustards.

Gorgonzola piccante contains less salt than its northern cousins, Roquefort and Stilton. It is creamier and less crumbly than the first, and milder than the second.

Grana Padano

The origins of Grana Padano can be traced back to around the year 1000, when the Cistercian monks of Chiaravalle in the province of Milan, invented the art of making Grana as a way of conserving their excess milk production. The success of Grana was so great that its consumption immediately spread throughout Italy. In fact, it appears in the kitchen archives of the government officials of Florence in 1334, as well as in a treatise on cheeses, written by Pantaleone da Confidenza in 1477, who called it *Piacentino*.

GRANA PADANO

MAIN PRODUCTION ZONES: southern Lombardy, Veneto, and Emilia Romagna (Po Valley)

AGING: 1–2 years

MADE FROM: skimmed cow's milk

FAT: 32%

SEASON: year round

TASTE: mild, almost sweet

Grana Padano

Grana takes its name from its grainy, often crumbly texture. Very easy to digest, it is a perfect after dinner cheese. It is also excellent served freshly grated over pasta and rice dishes, and can be used for cooking too. Wheels of Grana are quite large, varying in diameter from 14–18 in (35–45 cm) and are 7–10 in (18-25 cm) in height. They weigh between 55–88 lb (25–40 kg.)

Compact, grainy texture, is easy to flake off the wedge. It ranges in color from white to pale yellow. It gives off a sweet and fragrant odor.

Grano Padano should always be bought in wedges freshly cut from the wheel. They will be slightly moist and crumbly. Use any of the special little knives available to chip off elegant chunks when serving.

The Crust

The exterior is branded with a diamond shape trademark and the words "Grana Padano." After the aging process, each wheel is tested by officials who, armed with a small hammer, verify that when tapped, the correct sound is made, signifying the product quality. The crust is oiled during aging and is usually between $\frac{1}{6}$–$\frac{1}{3}$ in (4–8 mm) thick. It varies in color from golden-yellow to brown.

Thick yellow to brown crust.

Diamond shaped trade mark.

Regional production zone. This one comes from Padua.

Grana Padano "Ice Cream"
(Serves 4—6)

Ingredients
- 1 lb/500 g freshly grated Grana Padano cheese
- 4 cups/1 liter heavy/double cream
- salt and freshly ground white pepper to taste
- 7 oz/200 g Parma ham

In a double boiler, cook the cheese in the cream, without letting it come to the boil. Season with salt and pepper. When the mixture is creamy, set aside to cool. Pass through a sieve and transfer to an ice-cream maker, following the directions for traditional ice-cream. If you don't have an ice-cream maker, pour the mixture into a freezerproof container and freeze, stirring at intervals as the mixture thickens and freezes. After 3 hours in the freezer, transfer to a food processor and blend until smooth. Return to the freezer and repeat after another 3 hours. Serve with a platter of Parma ham.

Wine: a dry, sparkling red (Lambrusco)

Marzolino del Chianti

M arzolino has been made in Tuscany for centuries. During the Renaissance it was exported all over Europe. In the 16th century a doctor from Anverse praised the cheese for "its nutritional quality and refined flavor." Marzolino was originally only made from ewe's milk during the month of March (*Marzo*, in Italian, hence the name), when the ewes grazed on the first tender spring grasses. Nowadays it is made from a mixture of ewe's and cow's milk from fall through to late spring.

MARZOLINO DEL CHIANTI

MAIN PRODUCTION ZONE: Tuscany
AGING: about 40 days
MADE FROM: ewe's milk with additions of cow's milk
FAT: 40%
SEASON: October to May
TASTE: intense, piquant

Sweet Marzolino Pastries
(Serves 6)

Ingredients
- 2 rolls frozen puff pastry, thawed
- $1/2$ cup/125 ml butter, melted
- 4 oz/125 g Marzolino cheese, sliced
- 2 large pears, sliced
- 4 tbsp of sugar
- 1 tsp cinnamon
- 1 cup/125 g walnuts, chopped
- 1 tbsp unsweetened cocoa powder

Roll the pastry out into thin sheets, then cut it into pieces about 3 in/8 cm square. Brush them with half the butter. In the center of each piece, place a slice of cheese, then a slice of pear, and a teaspoon of sugar. Sprinkle with the cinnamon and walnuts. Fold the dough, forming triangular pockets and pinch the edges together to seal. Place the pastries on an oiled and floured baking tray sheet. Drizzle with the remaining butter, and sprinkle with the cocoa powder and a little extra sugar. Bake in a preheated oven at 400°F/200°C/gas 6 for about 30 minutes, or until the pastry is golden brown.

Wine: a dry red (Rosso di Montepulciano)

Thin, light yellow crust. The forms are shaped like chunky little wheels. Inside, the cheese is soft and white, with irregular pitting.

Serving Marzolino
In Tuscany, Marzolino is served with walnuts, pears, or honey. The coupling of cheeses with sweet foods is a Tuscan tradition. An allegorical painting of Envy presented at the carnival of Siena in 1719, shows *Cacio* (Pecorino cheese) being served with sweet foods.

Mascarpone

The name Mascarpone is said to be an adaptation of the Spanish *mas que bueno*, meaning "more than good," which one of the Spanish King's envoys is thought to have exclaimed after tasting it. Mascarpone was originally a by-product of *Crescenza* and *Stracchino* cheeses (see page 24–25), made from the excess cream extracted during their production. Today it is produced with pure cow's cream and looks more like a custard than a cheese. Mascarpone is widely used in cooking, especially in the preparation of desserts. It is delicious eaten plain or dusted with cocoa or coffee powder, either by itself or spread on cookies soaked in liqueur.

LOMBARDY

MASCARPONE

Main Production Zone: Lombardy
Aging: fresh
Made from: cow's milk cream
Fat content: 60%
Season: year round, although more is produced in winter
Taste: smooth and creamy

Mascarpone
It can be found in stores unpackaged at the cheese counters or in small packages of 3½-7 oz (100-200 g.) The consistency is that of a delicate custard, dense and compact. It is a yellowy-white color and has a sweet cream aroma. The flavor is smooth and sweet.

Tiramisu
(Serves 6)

Ingredients
- 5 eggs, separated
- ¾ cup/150 g superfine/caster sugar
- 1 lb/500 g Mascarpone cheese
- dash of salt
- 30 ladyfingers/sponge fingers
- 1 cup/250 ml strong espresso coffee
- 7 oz/200 g semi-sweet/dark chocolate, grated
- 1 tbsp unsweetened cocoa powder

Whisk the egg yolks and sugar until pale. Fold in the Mascarpone. Beat the egg whites with the salt until stiff and fold into the mixture. Spread a layer over the bottom of a large rectangular or oval dish. Dip the ladyfingers in the coffee and place a layer over the cream in the dish. Cover with a layer of the cream and sprinkle with a little chocolate. Repeat until all the ingredients are used up. Finish with a layer of cream and dust with the cocoa powder. Chill in the refrigerator for at least 4 hours before serving.

Wine: a dry, sparkling white (Asti Spumante Secco)

Mascarpone goes well with fresh fruit, but can also add subtlety and flavor to risottos and sauces.

Montasio

The origins of Montasio cheese date back over 700 years. They are attributed to the monks of the Abbey of Moggio whose pastures border the Montasio area of the Guilie Alps in Friuli. Montasio is a firm cheese, sold in three different ways depending on how long it has been aged: fresh, moderately aged, and aged. The first two make excellent table cheeses, while the aged variety is more suited to grating. Another variety of Montasio is known as *ubriaco* (which means "drunk" in Italian), because it is aged in pressed grapes.

MONTASIO

VENETO FRIULI-VENEZIA
Belluno GIULIA
Treviso
Padua Venice

Main production zones: Friuli-Venezia Giulia, Veneto (Belluno, Treviso, Padua, and Venice)

Aging: 2–5 months (fresh); 5–12 months (aged a little); 1 year + (aged)

Made from: cow's milk

Fat: 40%

Season: year round

Taste: delicate (fresh) strong, piquant (aged)

The Montasio consortium trademark is stamped onto the crust.

Shape and form

Forms of Montasio are about 12–18 in (30–40 cm) in diameter and 2½–4 in (6–10 cm) tall. They weigh from 11–20 lb (5–9 kg). The cheese itself is yellow or pale yellow, and this color intensifies with age.

Montasio Cheese Croutons
(Serves 4)

Ingredients
- 1½ tbsp butter
- 3 eggs
- 3½ oz/100 g freshly grated Montasio
- ¼ cup/30 g freshly grated Parmesan
- dash of nutmeg
- dash of salt

Beat the butter with an electric mixer until light and fluffy. Add the eggs, cheeses, nutmeg, and salt, while continuing to mix. Pour the mixture onto a baking sheet lined with waxed paper. Flatten to about ½ in/1 cm thick. Bake in a preheated oven at 350°F/180°C/gas 4 for 15 minutes, or until golden brown. When cool cut into squares. Serve with creamy vegetable soups.

Wine: a dry, sparkling red (Raboso Fiore)

Montasio brand name stamped onto the edges of the forms.

Mozzarella

Mozzarella is one of the most popular and versatile fresh cheeses. It is a basic ingredient in a wide variety of quintessentially Italian dishes, such as pizza, pasta salads, tomato and mozzarella salad (known as *Mozzarella in carrozza*, which means "Mozzarella in a carriage"), and a host of others. Originally, Mozzarella was made from water buffalo's milk in the Campania region (around Naples). As demand grew, there were not enough water buffalos to keep up the supply and cow's milk became more widely used. Nowadays cow's milk Mozzarella is cheaper and easier to find, although in recent years a number of *Mozzarella di buffala* "boutiques" have sprung up in many towns and cities.

MOZZARELLA

MAIN PRODUCTION ZONES: *traditionally, Campania, Lucania (Basilicata), Puglia, Lazio; nowadays, throughout Italy*
AGING: *fresh*
MADE FROM: *water buffalo's or cow's milk*
FAT: *varies, minimum 50%*
SEASON: *year round*
TASTE: *sweet, fresh, milky*

BURRATA

MAIN PRODUCTION ZONE: *Puglia*
AGING: *fresh*
MADE FROM: *cow's milk and cream*
FAT: *60%*
SEASON: *year round*
TASTE: *almost sweet, buttery*

Mozzarella is moist and springy to the touch. When cut, it will produce whey. It is porcelain white in color, with a barely perceptible (and completely edible) skin.

Mozzarella di bufala

Mozzarella made from water buffalo's milk is easily the best type available. While the cow's milk types are fine for cooking, nothing beats the extraordinary, almost musky flavor of the water buffalo milk variety when serving the cheese uncooked in salads. Although Mozzarella does not age well, it is often packaged in little plastic bags half filled with its own whey which allow the cheese a few more days of life.

Farfalle in a Spicy Tomato Sauce with Mozzarella

(Serves 4)

Ingredients
- 1–2 cloves garlic, finely chopped
- 1 tsp red pepper flakes
- 2 tbsp extra-virgin olive oil
- 2 lb/1 kg cherry tomatoes, cut in half
- salt and freshly ground black pepper to taste
- 1 tbsp capers
- 5 basil leaves
- 1 lb/500 g farfalle pasta
- 4 oz/125 g Mozzarella cheese, diced

Sauté the garlic in the oil. Add the tomatoes, red pepper flakes, salt and pepper. Cover and cook over low heat for 15 minutes. Add the capers and basil and cook for 10 minutes more. Meanwhile, cook the pasta in a large pot of salted, boiling water until *al dente*. Drain, and toss with the sauce and Mozzarella. Let the pasta sit for a few minutes before serving.

Wine: a dry white (Frascati Superiore)

Bocconcini can be served whole in salads and pasta dishes.

Garnish this tasty pasta dish with sprigs of bright green fresh basil.

Bocconcini
The traditional shape for Mozzarella is a roundish ball about the size of a fist, but it also comes in braids and small bite-size pieces called *bocconcini* (little mouthfuls) or *ciliegini* (little cherries). Whatever the shape, the outer surface is always smooth and porcelain white. The interior is white and when the Mozzarella is fresh it should produce milky beads of whey when sliced. Traditionally, Mozzarella was not conserved in its whey as it is today, but was wrapped in reed or myrtle leaves.

The story of Mozzarella
The original Mozzarella, made from water buffalo's milk, is documented as far back as the 13th century by monks in the town of Capua, who fed *pane e mozza* (bread and Mozzarella) to weary pilgrims. Some food historians claim that water buffalo farming dates back to Roman times, whereas others say that water buffalo were introduced to Italy during the Norman occupation of Sicily. The Mozzarella industry was born in the 17th century when the first *bufalare* (Mozzarella producers) are recorded.

Tomato and Mozzarella Salad

(Serves 4)

Ingredients
- 6–8 large, ripe salad tomatoes
- 1 lb/500 g Mozzarella cheese (preferably made with water buffalo's milk)
- 20 fresh basil leaves, torn
- salt and freshly ground black pepper to taste
- 6 tbsp extra-virgin olive oil

Cut the tomatoes into ¼-in/5-mm thick slices. Cut the Mozzarella in slices of the same thickness. Arrange the slices alternately on an attractive serving dish. Sprinkle with the basil, salt, and pepper, and drizzle with the oil.

Wine: a dry white (Est! Est! Est!)

The success of this simple salad depends on the quality of the ingredients. Make sure the olive oil is fresh and bright green in color.

Mozzarella, tomato, and basil are often served together in Italy. Their colors combined make up the green/white/red of the Italian flag.

Fior di Latte

The more widely-available cow's milk Mozzarella is known as *Fior di latte*, which means "flower of milk" (right). Almost identical in appearance to water buffalo's milk Mozzarella, it lacks some of the latter's delicacy of flavor and is best used in cooking.

Mozzarella affumicata

Since Mozzarella only lasts a few days, it is often smoked so that it will keep longer. Smoked Mozzarella is usually shaped in the form of a braid or oval and it takes on a lovely deep gold exterior color and a warm yellow interior. Its complex smokey flavor makes it ideal as a sandwich filling or as an antipasto.

Burnished gold exterior and warm yellow, smooth interior.

A braid of pure white Mozzarella makes an eyecatching addition to a selection of antipasti or the after-dinner cheese board.

Treccia

All Mozzarella is made using the same *pasta filata* (layering) method, where the curds are cut into strips, then covered in boiling water. As they rise to the surface, they are torn into shreds and then pressed into balls or long "sausages" which are then braided into *treccia* (braids). The flavor is the same.

Burrata

Burrata is a relatively modern specialty from Puglia; it was invented in Andria at the beginning of the 20th century. It must be eaten very fresh, no more than 48 hours after production. The casing of the Burrata, formed by some of the spun Mozzarella, is filled with some of the unspun curd along with fresh cream and milk enzymes.

Burrata cheese is wrapped in the sturdy blades of a local herb which flavors the cheese with its pungent aroma.

Murazzano

Murazzano is a fresh cheese that belongs to the Robiola family. It takes its name from the tiny commune of Murazzano and thereabouts, where small quantities are produced by local cheesemakers. It is a very old cheese and its production technique is even mentioned in Pliny the Elder's *Naturalis Historia*. It can be made with 100 percent ewe's milk (in which case the forms are marked *di latte di pecora*), or with a combination of ewe's and cow's milk. It is a perfect table cheese.

MURAZZANO

MAIN PRODUCTION ZONES: Piedmont (Cuneo, Murazzano)

AGING: 7–10 days

MADE FROM: at least 40% ewe's milk, with additional cow's milk.

FAT: 53%

SEASON: year round

TASTE: delicate, with a herbal aftertaste

SERVING MURAZZANO
This delicate cheese can be served as it is, or with a light drizzle of olive oil and a grinding of black pepper.

Trade mark.

The animals whose milk is used to make Murazzano are fed exclusively on fresh grass and hay.

During the brief aging period the forms are washed daily with warm water. This forms a very light crust.

Murazzano Cream Cheese with Fresh Herbs

(Serves 4)

Ingredients
- 2 cloves garlic, finely chopped
- 1 lb/500 g Murazzano cheese
- 1 bay leaf
- 1 tbsp onion, finely chopped
- 1 tsp each fresh basil, thyme, sage, chopped
- 2 tsp of heavy/double cream
- 1 tbsp extra-virgin olive oil

Mix all the ingredients together in a blender. Place the resulting cream in the refrigerator for at least two hours prior to serving. Spread on toast or crackers.

Wine: a light, dry white (Gavi)

Parmigiano Reggiano

Parmesan is the King of Italian cheeses and perhaps the best known internationally. However, what is known generically as Parmesan abroad, has different names and production areas in Italy. Parmigiano Reggiano, considered the best variety, is produced in just four localities in Emilia (Bologna, Modena, Reggio-Emilia and Parma) and one in Lombardy (Mantua). It is certainly an old cheese, since Boccaccio mentions it in his 14th century *Decameron*. There are strict laws governing its production and the addition of preservatives is strictly forbidden.

PARMIGIANO REGGIANO

PRODUCTION ZONES: Bologna, Modena, Reggio-Emilia, Parma, Mantua

AGING: 1–4 years

MADE FROM: skimmed cow's milk. The cows must be fed only on fresh grass or hay.

FAT: 32%.

SEASON: year round

TASTE: intense

Month and year of production.

Consortium brand name for quality guarantee.

The best Parmigiano Reggiano

Parmigiano Reggiano is made in small cheese factories on the Po River plain. It is claimed that the very best variety is made during the spring and fall in the Enza River Valley on the border between the provinces of Parma and Reggio-Emilia.

Producer's number.

The outer crust of Parmigiano Reggiano is clearly marked with the production date, the form number, and the area in which it was produced.

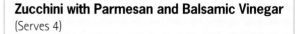

Zucchini with Parmesan and Balsamic Vinegar
(Serves 4)

Ingredients
- 2 large zucchini/courgettes
- 4 oz/125 g Parmesan cheese, flaked
- 2 tbsp Balsamic vinegar

Thinly slice the zucchini and arrange on a serving dish. Cover with the flakes of Parmesan cheese. Drizzle with the Balsamic vinegar and serve.

Wine: a dry, lightly sparkling white (Colli Piacentini Sauvignon Frizzante)

Special little Parmesan knives and forks are ideal for cutting and chipping flakes from the wedge.

Parmigiano Reggiano
Parmesan should always be brought in a wedge-shaped piece newly cut from the form. Grate it freshly to sprinkle over pasta; there are a number of small hand-held graters available now that can be placed on the table so that diners can help themselves.

The compact, grainy texture is ideal for grating or chipping off flakes to serve at the table. Color varies from straw yellow to pale gold.

Pecorino

Pecorino cheese, made with ewe's milk, is produced throughout most of central and southern Italy and the islands. Characteristics vary according to the area of production. It is one of the oldest cheeses in Italy, since sheep were kept for milk and cheese production long before cows. It is widely produced, and in the more isolated villages of the Apennines and the south "Pecorino" is synonymous with "cheese." Most regions produce more than one type. Tuscany, Lazio, Sicily, and Sardinia produce some of the best Pecorino.

PECORINO

MAIN PRODUCTION ZONES: central and southern Italy and the islands.
AGING: from 2 months to 3 years.
MADE FROM: ewe's milk.
FAT: 48%.
SEASON: year round
TASTE: sharp and spicy in the aged varieties; creamy and pungent in the younger varieties; sweet and intense in the Tuscan varieties.

Pecorino with Pears
(Serves 4)

Ingredients
- 8 oz/250 g fresh Pecorino cheese
- 2 large ripe pears

Slice the Pecorino in thick wedges. Slice and, if you wish, core the pears. Arrange on an attractive dish and serve.
Wine: a light, dry white (Chardonnay)

Pecorino di Pienza preserved in olive oil
The area around Pienza in central Tuscany is known for its Pecorino preserved in extra-virgin olive oil aromatized with local herbs. Sealed in glass jars, the cheese is aged in the oil. It will keep for about 12 months.

Pecorino romano is now made by hundreds of different producers. Some are tiny local factories, others gather milk over huge areas and produce it on an industrial scale. Overall, the quality is excellent.

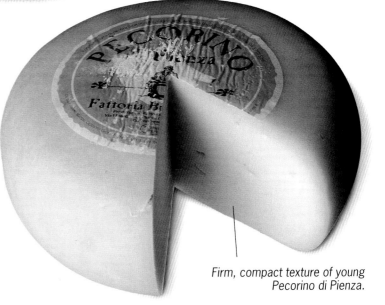

Hard, grainy texture of mature Pecorino. Similar in appearance to Parmesan.

Pecorino romano

Despite its name, and due to the huge increase in demand, most Pecorino romano is now produced outside the province of Rome, in southern Tuscany and Sardinia. The latter is judged to be of highest quality. Its high salt content and strong, spicy flavor make it an ideal grating cheese. It can also be served in flakes to finish a meal. It is aged for 4–12 months.

The crust is often coated with a mixture of olive oil and tomato, giving it an orangy color.

Pecorino di Pienza

This Pecorino is produced in the beautiful valleys and hills of southern Tuscany around the Renaissance town of Pienza. It has a strong, intense flavor and, like other Tuscan Pecorino, is sweet rather than spicy. Aged for 1–2 months, it is sold as *fresco* (fresh), while after 3–6 months it is called *stagionato* (aged). Both are excellent table cheeses.

Firm, compact texture of young Pecorino di Pienza.

Pecorino di fossa

In the area around Siena (including Pienza), Pecorino is often aged underground, sometimes wrapped in walnut leaves or buried in ash or other substances for extra flavor. Further south, at Talamello in the Marches, the Pecorino is wrapped in walnut leaves and aged in the local tufo caves. The day the caves are opened in November is a local holiday.

Crust labeled "Formaggio di fossa."

Firm compact texture. The aromatic herbs that grow wild in the hills of the Pienza region add flavor and distinction to the ewe's milk which is used to make the local cheeses.

Pecorino and fava beans

The new season's earliest fava (broad) beans arrive in the markets of Florence in February and throughout the spring months fresh, raw fava beans are served with young Pecorino as starters or at the end of the meal in Tuscan homes and restaurants. Try it!

Scoperino

Scoperino is another delicious Tuscan Pecorino. It is aged in caves, where the humidity causes the crust to crinkle and crack.

Most of the aged varieties of Pecorino siciliano are flavored with whole grains of black pepper.

Pecorino siciliano

Homer makes mention of Pecorino siciliano in his epic poem the *Odyssey* (which dates to some time before 800 BC!), when he describes Polyphemos preparing blocks of cheese and putting them in baskets. The best known modern versions of Pecorino siciliano are *Primo sale*, which is salted only once and aged for 4 months, and *Pepato*, characterized by the addition of black pepper, according to the Arab tradition.

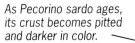

As Pecorino sardo ages, its crust becomes pitted and darker in color.

Mild Pecorino sardo is aged for 3 months and is served as a table cheese. The mature variety is aged for more than 8 months and can either be served at table or used as a grating cheese. The texture of the aged Pecorino is compact and flaky.

Pecorino sardo

Pecorino sardo, known until just a few years ago as *semicotto* (half cooked), is made in two different versions: mild and mature. The typical mild version has a light and smooth outer layer, while the cheese itself is soft and white with a smooth flavor. The mature version, aged for longer, has a darker crust while the interior tends to become more yellow as it ages, as well as becoming increasingly piquant in flavor. Some smoked varieties of Pecorino sardo also exist.

Soup with Pecorino Sardo
(Serves 6)

Ingredients
- 4 oz/125 g mild Pecorino sardo cheese, thinly sliced
- 12 slices toasted bread
- 2 quarts/2 liters beef stock
- salt and freshly ground black pepper

In a large ovenproof baking dish, arrange alternating layers of Pecorino and toast. Finish with a layer of cheese. Pour the hot stock over top and cook in a preheated oven at 400°F/200°C/gas 6 for about 20 minutes. Serve hot.

Wine: a dry red (Cannonau di Sardegna)

Serving Pecorino
All varieties of fresh, young Pecorino are good table cheeses. Their salty flavor goes especially well with bread, making them excellent for sandwiches. The older cheeses are also good for the table, particularly if you like a strong, spicy bite in your cheese. The aged varieties make excellent grating cheeses, and can be served over pasta and a host of other dishes.

The crust of this Pecorino sardo shows the imprints of the basket in which it was aged. Forms of Pecorino sardo weigh between 9–26 lb (4–12 kg).

47

Buying and storing pecorino
Always buy all your Italian cheeses from a reputable delicatessen or specialty store. When buying cheeses like Pecorino that are produced in forms, insist that the wedge you buy is cut from the form before your eyes. That way you will know that it is fresh. Young Pecorino will keep in the refrigerator for several days if well wrapped in foil. The aged varieties will keep for up to 2 weeks.

Provolone

Like Mozzarella, Provolone is made by the *pasta filata* (layering) process, which gives it its classically smooth texture. Originally a southern cheese, most of the Provolone produced in Italy today is made in the north. There are two types of Provolone — *dolce*, which is aged for 2 months, and *piccante*, aged for about 12 months. The few types of Provolone produced in the south today are generally much stronger and spicier than the northern varieties.

PROVOLONE

MAIN PRODUCTION ZONES: Lombardy, Emilia Romagna (Cremona, Brescia, Piacenza)

AGING: 2 months for dolce (mild) and 12 months for piccante (mature)

MADE FROM: whole cow's milk

FAT: 45%

SEASON: year round

TASTE: sweet and buttery (dolce) and intense and spicy (piccante)

Provolone dolce

The mild or "sweet" variety is younger and paler in color. It is generally made with 100 percent cow's milk. Its smooth, almost silky texture and delicate flavor make it an ideal table cheese. The young cheese is cream to pale yellow in color, with only very limited and tiny pitting. The smooth yellow crust is generally marked *dolce*.

Year of production.

Provolone is made in many different shapes and sizes (some enormous), including rounds, ovals, sausage-shaped, and pear-shaped. This form of Provolone Auricchio has been given a classic melon shape by the string used to hang it during the aging process.

Cabbage and Provolone Soup
(Serves 6)

Ingredients
- 3 tbsp butter
- 2 cloves garlic, finely chopped
- 1 onion, finely chopped
- 5 oz/150 g pancetta/unsmoked bacon, diced
- 1 small cabbage, cut into strips
- 6 cups/1.5 liters boiling vegetable stock
(prepare with hot water and a stock cube)
- salt and freshly ground black pepper
- 6 slices firm-textured bread, toasted
- 6 oz/180 g Provolone piccante, thinly sliced

Melt the butter in a large, heavy-bottomed saucepan and sauté the garlic, onion, and pancetta until golden. Add the cabbage, cover, and cook for 5 minutes more. Pour in the stock and cook for 15 minutes. Add salt and pepper to taste. Place a slice of toast at the bottom of each of six individual soup bowls and cover with the cheese. Ladle the hot soup over the bread and cheese and serve.

Wine: a dry red (Ischia Rosso)

Provolone piccante
The strongest, southern Provolones are aged for up to 12 months. Many are made with a mixture of cow's, goat's, and ewe's, or even water buffalo's milk. If you are ever in Naples, be sure to order a *panino con Provolone piccante* (sandwich with Provolone piccante). The very chewy local bread and the spicy cheese form a perfect partnership.

Provolone darkens with age and the pitting becomes more obvious.

Many of the milder Provolone cheeses are smoked, which turns their crusts a beautiful burnished gold color. The smooth, musky flavor of smoked Provolone is divine.

Quartirolo

Quartirolo cheese is named after the grass (called *quartirola*) on which the cow's grazed at the end of summer when they returned from the alpine pastures. The cheese belongs to the Stracchino family and in the past was known as *Stracchino Quadro* (Square Stracchino). Nowadays Quartirolo is sold either as a young *pasta tenera* cheese or a slightly aged *maturo* version. There is also a low-fat type made with skimmed milk. Quartirolo is a good table cheese and goes well with salads and walnuts.

QUARTIROLO

MAIN PRODUCTION ZONE: Lombardy
AGING: 5–40 days
MADE FROM: cow's milk
FAT: 30%
SEASON: traditionally, fall and winter, now year round
TASTE: slightly acidic, but acquires intensity and fragrance with aging

Be sure to serve these delicious pastry puffs straight from the oven. If there are any leftover, warm them up again before serving the next day.

Quartirolo Cheese Appetizers
(Serve 4–6)

Ingredients
- 4 oz/125 g Quartirolo cheese, cubed
- 1 tbsp finely chopped parsley,
- 3 oz/90 g freshly grated Parmesan cheese
- 3 eggs
- freshly ground black pepper to taste
- 1 lb/500 g puff pastry
- 2 oz/60 g butter, melted

Mix the Quartirolo, parsley, Parmesan, eggs, and pepper together in a large bowl. Roll the puff pastry out until very thin then cut into squares about 4 in/10 cm wide. Brush with half the melted butter. In the center of each pastry square, place one tablespoon of the cheese mixture and fold the dough over it to form a triangular shape. Pinch the edges to seal well. Place on a greased baking sheet. Brush with the remaining butter and bake in a preheated oven at 400°F/200°C/gas 6 for about 30 minutes, or until golden brown. Serve hot.

Wine: a light, dry white (Bianco di Custoza)

Quartirolo maturo

In order to qualify as Quartirolo maturo, the cheese must be aged for about 30 days. This older version of Quartirolo is slightly darker in color and is flaky with a stronger, more aromatic flavor. It also develops a darker crust, changing from light gold to dark brown as the weeks go by.

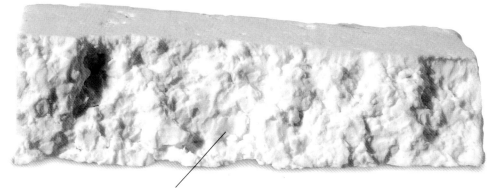

The mature version of Quartirolo is flaky with larger pitting than the fresh variety.

Quartirolo a pasta tenera

After just five days of aging, Quartirolo *a pasta tenera* is ready to be sold. This variety is white or cream-colored with a delicate, almost sweet flavor. Its creamy texture melts in the mouth. Previously, the aged version was preferred to the younger variety, but this has changed in recent years.

Creamy texture and white color are typical of the fresh Quartirolo. Some slight pitting.

Light yellow crust.

Box in which the cheese is aged.

Shape and production

Quartirolo is an excellent table cheese and comes in a classic square shape. The forms vary in weight from 2–9lb (1-4 kg) and in height from 1¾–3 in (4-8 cm.) Many are aged in wooden cartons with reed bases for the air to pass through. Quartirolo is also known as *Stracchino di Milano*.

Ricotta

icotta (which means "recooked" and refers to the production method) is made throughout Italy. The ancient Romans are known to have made Ricotta, although it didn't become widespread until the Middle Ages. Nowadays, every region produces Ricotta in one form or another and there are many different varieties. Fresh Ricotta has a very delicate flavor and should be consumed the same day it is bought.

RICOTTA FRESCA

MAIN PRODUCTION ZONES: *Piedmont, Veneto, Emilia-Romagna, Lazio, Puglia, Calabria, Sicily, and Sardinia*

AGING: *fresh*

MADE FROM: *cow's milk, mixed cow's and ewe's milk, or, more rarely, ewe's or goat's milk*

FAT: *10%*

SEASON: *year round*

TASTE: *very delicate*

Ricotta has no crust. It is white, slightly granular, and not compact. If not eaten when very fresh it quickly becomes acidic.

52

Fresh Ricotta

Most commercially produced Ricotta is made from cow's milk, or mixed cow's and ewe's milk. It only lasts a few days and should be stored in the refrigerator. Most supermarkets now sell plastic containers of Ricotta; this is generally of inferior quality, although it does keep for longer.

Making Ricotta

Ricotta is made by reheating the whey leftover when making hard cheeses. Soft and pure white, milk or even cream are sometimes added to improve consistency. The freshly made cheeses are put into little baskets (nowadays made of plastic) to drain.

The baskets used to drain the forms of Ricotta leave characteristic markings on the surface of the fresh cheese.

Florentine Style Crêpes

(Serves 6–8)

Ingredients

For the pancakes:
- 1½ cups/325 ml milk
- 1 cup/150 g flour
- 3 eggs
- 1 tsp salt
- 4 tbsp water

For the filling:
- 1 clove garlic, finely chopped
- 3 tbsp extra-virgin olive oil
- 2 cups/500 g boiled and chopped spinach
- salt and freshly ground pepper to taste
- dash of nutmeg
- 5 oz/150 g Ricotta cheese
- 3 tbsp freshly grated Parmesan cheese

For the sauce:
- 4 tbsp extra-virgin olive oil
- ½ cup/75 g flour
- 2 cups/500 ml milk
- salt and freshly ground black pepper to taste
- dash of nutmeg
- 3 tbsp freshly grated Parmesan cheese

TO MAKE THE CRÊPES: place the flour in a medium bowl and gradually pour in the milk, beating vigorously. Add the eggs, salt, and water and beat until smooth. Leave to rest for half an hour. Grease a skillet (frying pan) or crêpe pan and place over medium heat. Pour in half a ladleful of the batter and move the pan so that the batter spreads evenly over the bottom. As soon as the crêpe sets, flip it and cook the other side. Repeat, stacking the cooked crêpes in a pile.

FOR THE FILLING: sauté the garlic in the oil, add the spinach, salt, pepper, and nutmeg. Remove from the heat and mix with the Ricotta and Parmesan.

FOR THE SAUCE: heat the oil, and add the flour stirring constantly. Add the milk gradually, still stirring, until the mixture boils and thickens. Add salt, pepper, nutmeg, and the Parmesan cheese. Put a generous line of filling on each pancake. Roll them up and arrange in an oiled oven-proof dish. Pour the sauce over the top. Bake in a preheated oven at 400°F/200°C/gas 6 until the top is golden. Serve hot.

Wine: a light, dry white (Gavi or Malvasia Istriana)

Cooking with Ricotta

Fresh Ricotta can be served on its own as a table cheese. It can be served as a dessert, with the addition of a little sugar and vanilla extract (essence), grated chocolate, fruit, and a variety of other sweeteners, and is an essential ingredient in cheesecake. Widely used in Italian cooking; its very mild flavor combines well with spinach, Swiss chard, herbs, black pepper, and nutmeg (to name a few).

Ricotta is classically associated with spinach, especially in the filling for ravioli, but also in a number of pies and other preparations.

Ricotta Salata

Ricotta salata (salted Ricotta) is made by adding salt to the fresh Ricotta mixture to preserve it. This allows the cheese to be aged for many months. Ricotta salata can be served as a table cheese, used in cooking, and, when suitably aged, for grating over pasta dishes in place of Pecorino or Parmesan. Other methods of conserving Ricotta include baking it in the oven, cooking it the cinders of an open fire, and even, in Sicily, drying it in the sun.

RICOTTA SALATA

MAIN PRODUCTION ZONE: southern Italy
AGING: 2-12 months
MADE FROM: cow's or ewe's milk
Fat: 38%
SEASON: year round
TASTE: sharp and salty

PUGLIA
CAMPANIA
BASILICATA
SARDINIA
CAMPANIA
SICILY

Baked Ricotta turns a light golden brown on the inside and a much darker brown outside.

Brown crust, with a little ash still showing.

Ricotta infornata

Sicily is famous for Ricotta infornata (Baked Ricotta), which is made by baking fresh or salted Ricotta in the oven. The fresh Ricotta is placed in large pans, salted, and sprinkled with ground black pepper. It is then baked until a brown crust forms on top. Salted Ricotta is baked and can be either eaten at once or kept as a grating cheese. Sultanas, chocolate, or candied fruit are sometimes added to Baked Ricotta, to make a sweet dessert cheese.

Ricotta cotta sulla brace

Traditionally, fresh Ricotta was also cooked in the last embers of an open fire. This method preserved the cheese, allowing it to be kept for several months.

Firm, compact texture of Ricotta salata from Sardinia.

Ricotta salata

In order to produce Ricotta salata, molds of fresh Ricotta are spread with dry salt every 24 to 48 hours. This process is repeated two or three times. During the aging process, the outer shell is carefully cleaned to avoid the formation of any mold spores.

Mold pores form very quickly on the crust and must be cleaned off.

Pasta Salad with Ricotta and Arugula
(Serves 4)

Ingredients
- 1 lb/500 g fusilli pasta
- 6 tbsp extra-virgin olive oil
- 3 cloves garlic, finely chopped
- 4 ripened tomatoes, seeded and diced
- ½ cup/60 g pitted black olives
- 12 oz/350 g fresh Ricotta cheese
- 2 oz/60 g arugula/rocket, thinly sliced
- 2 oz/60 g salted Ricotta cheese, in flakes

Boil the fusilli in a large pot of salted, boiling water. When cooked *al dente,* run under cold water. Drain well, pat dry ith a clean tea towel, and transfer to a large serving bowl. Combine the oil, garlic, tomatoes, fresh Ricotta, and arugula and toss well. Pour the sauce into the bowl with the pasta and toss well. Sprinkle with the salted Ricotta and chill in the refrigerator for about 2 hours. Remove the pasta from the refrigerator one hour before serving.

Wine: a medium white (Malvasia Istriana)

Robiola

R obiola is a generic name for a number of fresh cheeses, most of which are produced in Piedmont and Lombardy. It is very ancient; the Ligurian Celts produced a similar cheese, and Pliny the Elder praised its qualities in his *Naturalis Historia*. Originally Robiola was made from goat's milk (when it was still considered a poor man's food), whereas most modern Robiolas are made from cow's milk or a mixture of cow's, ewe's, and/or goat's milk. Robiola di Roccaverano is the noblest of the modern types and the only one to carry the government guarantees (D.O.C. and D.O.P.). Bruss, made with leftover Robiola, is a strong, unusual cheese, renowned, among other things, for its properties as an aphrodisiac.

ROBIOLA

MAIN PRODUCTION ZONES: Piedmont, Lombardy

AGING: 3-20 days

MADE FROM: 80% cow's milk with additions of goat's and/or ewe's milk

FAT: about 45%

SEASON: year round

TASTE: sweet, delicate

Robiola of Roccaverano forms are small and cylindrical, weighing about 10–13 oz (300–400 g).

Robiola
Creamy, fresh Robiola is widely available in supermarkets throughout Italy in small square forms.

Robiola of Roccaverano
Robiola of Roccaverano, produced in several mountain villages in the provinces of Alessandria and Asti, is the best known type of Robiola. It is made according to strict government regulations: the animals whose milk is used must only be fed on fresh grass and hay, and the milk must be aged for at least three days at a temperature between 60–70°F (15–20°C.) Some Robiola of Roccaverano is aged wrapped in cabbage leaves; the humidity they produce makes this type especially creamy.

Bruss

Bruss, a creamy cheese of exceptional strength and flavor, is produced in Piedmont. It is made with pieces (or leftovers from the production) of Robiola, mixed with grappa (or white wine), black pepper, and chilli pepper. This mixture is covered with extra-virgin olive oil and left to rest for 2–3 days, then mixed again and left in a warm, sheltered place for a further 25 days.

Bruss is sold in terra-cotta or glass jars. It is served on slices of bread at the end of lunch or dinner. Bruss is related to Fromage fort produced in the south of France.

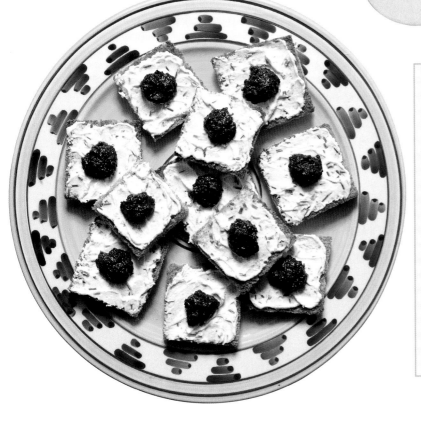

Robiola and Olive Toasts
(Serves 4)

Ingredients
- 4 oz/125 g Robiola cheese
- 1 tbsp finely chopped fresh chives
- 2 oz/60 g pitted black olives
- 2 anchovy fillets
- 1 tsp capers conserved in vinegar
- 2 tbsp extra-virgin olive oil
- 8 slices whole wheat/wholemeal bread with crusts removed, cut into squares and toasted

Mix the Robiola with the chives. In a blender or food processor, finely chop the olives, anchovies, capers, and oil. Spread the Robiola on the toast and top each with a teaspoonful of the olive oil mixture.

Wine: a light, dry white (Verdicchio Castelli di Jesi)

Scamorza

Scamorza is a spun cheese, belonging to the same family as Mozzarella and Provolone. Like Provolone, it is shaped like a pear (although the forms are smaller). Although Scamorza is much drier than Mozzarella, it still very smooth in texture. It is firm to the cut, white, and buttery. Scamorza is generally eaten fresh or smoked, but there are also a few slightly aged varieties.

SCAMORZA

MAIN PRODUCTION ZONES: southern Italy, especially Abruzzi, Molise, and Basilicata

AGING: minimum of 7 days

Made from: cow's milk

FAT: 38%

SEASON: year round

TASTE: sweet and delicate

Smoked Scamorza

The smoked version has a lovely burnished gold outer layer. It is an excellent table cheese and is also used in cooking. It is especially good when roasted over a barbecue or grill.

Forms of Scamorza are tied together in pairs and hung during aging. This produces their characteristic pear shape.

Grilled Zucchini with Smoked Scamorza

(Serves 2)

Ingredients
- 6 zucchini/courgettes, sliced very thinly
- 3 tbsp extra-virgin olive oil
- 1 tsp of apple cider vinegar
- salt and freshly ground black pepper to taste
- 6 fresh mint leaves, torn
- 3 oz/90 g smoked Scamorza cheese, thinly sliced

Arrange the zucchini in a well-oiled ovenproof baking dish. In a bowl, whisk the oil with the vinegar, salt, and pepper until well blended. Pour over the zucchini, and then sprinkle with the mint. Bake in a preheated oven at 400°F/200°C/gas 6 for about 20 minutes, turning the slices frequently. Then, arrange the cheese slices in the center of the dish and bake for 5 more minutes, or until the cheese is melted and golden brown. Serve hot.

Wine: a light, dry or aromatic white (Trebbiano di Romagna, Gewürztraminer)

Taleggio

Taleggio is the recent name (it appears for the first time in 1918) for this cheese, which has been produced in Lombardy for many centuries. Before then, it was known as *Stracchino* (like most of the soft cheeses from Lombardy). Taleggio is a table cheese, with a firm, creamy consistency and a light aromatic flavor.

TALEGGIO

MAIN PRODUCTION ZONES: *Lombardy and Veneto*
AGING: *about 40 days*
MADE FROM: *cow's milk*
FAT: *48%*
SEASON: *year round*
TASTE: *full and aromatic*

Thin, soft crust, light gold in color which deepens as the cheese ages.

Taleggio is produced in square or rectangular forms about 8 in (20 cm) long and 2–2¹/₂ in (5–6 cm) in height. The outer crust is soft, slightly wrinkled, and pale gold in color. Inside, the cheese is a creamy yellow and denser in the center. It is one of Italy's best table cheeses.

59

Tomatoes Stuffed with Taleggio
(Serves 4)

Ingredients
- 8 ripe tomatoes
- salt and freshly ground black pepper to taste
- 4 tbsp extra-virgin olive oil
- 5 tbsp flour
- 2 cups/500 ml milk
- dash of nutmeg
- 4 oz/125 g Taleggio cheese, diced
- 1 tbsp finely chopped parsley
- 1 tbsp finely chopped basil

Cut the tomatoes in half, squeezing gently to remove the seeds. Sprinkle with a little salt and lay them upside down on a cutting board to drain. Heat 3 tablespoons of the oil in a small saucepan, then add the flour, stirring constantly with a wooden spoon until the mixture thickens. Then, over low heat, slowly add the milk, stirring continuously. Cook until the mixture is smooth and dense. Add the salt, pepper, nutmeg, and cheese and stir until the cheese has melted. Place the tomatoes in an ovenproof baking dish and season lightly with salt and pepper. Drizzle with the remaining oil, and sprinkle with the parsley and basil. Bake in a preheated oven at 400°F/200°C/gas 6 for 20 minutes. Fill the tomatoes with the cheese sauce and cook for 20 minutes more.

Wine: a dry, fruit white (Pinot Bianco)

Toma

T oma is an ancient cheese; it is mentioned in the Treatise of Turin dating to 1477. The exact origin of the name is vague, but it may be derived from the Provençal *tuomo,* a word which in the local dialect means "form." Toma is produced in two different varieties, regular and low-fat. Regular Toma is an excellent table cheese, as well as the main ingredient in some special local polenta dishes. The low-fat version is exclusively a table cheese.

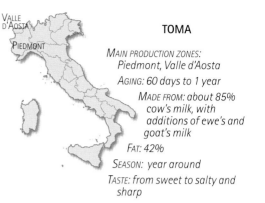

TOMA

MAIN PRODUCTION ZONES:
Piedmont, Valle d'Aosta

AGING: 60 days to 1 year

MADE FROM: about 85% cow's milk, with additions of ewe's and goat's milk

FAT: 42%

SEASON: year around

TASTE: from sweet to salty and sharp

After 1 month of aging the crust is light yellow and reasonably smooth; it becomes progressively darker and more wrinkly as it ages.

60

Young Toma is light yellow in color with small pitting. It darkens with age and the pitting becomes more pronounced.

Toma is produced in small forms about 6–10 in (15–25 cm) in diameter and 2–4 in (5–10 cm) in height. They weigh anywhere between 2–9 lb (1–4¹⁄₂ kg.)

Rice with Tasty Toma
(Serves 4)

Ingredients
- 11 oz/300 g short-grain rice
- 4 oz/125 g Toma cheese, cubed
- 4 tbsp butter
- dash of salt

Boil the rice in salted water until cooked *al dente*. Drain the rice, conserving some of the cooking water in a small bowl. Add the cheese to the rice together with a little of the cooking water. Stir until the cheese is melted. Add the butter, and salt to taste, mix again, and serve.

Wine: a full-bodied, dry red (Merlot del Collio)

Potato, Pancetta, and Toma Casserole
(Serves 4)

Ingredients
- 2 tbsp extra-virgin olive oil
- 8 large potatoes, thinly sliced
- salt and freshly ground black pepper to taste
- 4 oz/125 g lean pancetta/unsmoked bacon, thinly sliced
- 5 oz/150 g Toma cheese, sliced

Sauté the potatoes in the oil until half-cooked. Season with salt and pepper and remove from the heat. Layer an ovenproof baking dish with the pancetta, followed by a layer of the potatoes, leaving the the pancetta at the sides of the dish uncovered so that it will go crispy. Bake in a preheated oven at 400°F/200°C/gas 6 for about 20 minutes. Remove from the oven and cover with the cheese, then return to the oven and cook until the cheese has melted.

Wine: a full-bodied, dry red (Dolcetto d'Alba)

Index

Credits

The Publishers would like to thank

Baroni (Florence), Dino Bartolini (Florence)
C.I.D.A. Srl (Florence), Cardelli e Gagliotti (Florence)
Mastrociliegia (Fiesole, Florence)
who kindly lent props for the photography.

All photos by Marco Lanza and Walter Mericchi except:

Farabolafoto, Milan: 10 BL, 11 TR, Giuliano Cappelli, Florenz: 10 TL
Giuseppe Carfagna, Rom: 6 BL, 8 TL, 9 TR, 9 TL, 9 B
Overseas, Mailand: 8 BL, 8 R